Reflection

Reflection

Tim Bright

Library of Congress Control Number:		2017905425
ISBN:	Hardcover	978-1-5434-1413-4
	Softcover	978-1-5434-1411-0
	eBook	978-1-5434-1412-7

Print information available on the last page.

Rev. date: 04/27/2017

To order additional copies of this book, contact:
Xlibris
1-888-795-4274
www.Xlibris.com
Orders@Xlibris.com
759841

Contents

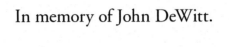

In memory of John DeWitt.

The Door

If the door were open I
would climb this mountain
to gaze at scudding clouds.

I don't intend to show the way,
but watch the flowers of this mountain
bloom and the leaves fall from its
trees.

Where is the door; where should it
be?

Furniture in the tiny house rearranges
itself. In the ravine a blind man sees
his sheep.

Far away from the mountain I observe a
bridge standing strong against a storm; the sea
succumbing to the land.

Mystical structure is not the only thing
that keeps me in the game. If the door
opens I will climb this mountain.

An Error

I don't know if they care
if it's a land or a world, dressed
to go; their backs the spine of
a sea worm. Dressed for the world,
dressed to go. What a frightening
thing they are when I see them on
a sidewalk, their shoes like pails.

What is a land to them or a village,
something to walk on, clucking at
a sky? Their friends are a beehive
of let's go.

I see them walking on a land—
giant chickens out for a stroll, their
clothes plaid green and brown
intersecting where a branch joins
a tree.

To concerts they go, a magnet to
their heart, gray hair fluffing in
still air. Crazy is the piano and violins
shaking the land, while they twirl
in hysteria at such beauty let's go.

Blue Man

Watching a blue man skip
on a telephone wire reminds
me of when I walked from The George
Washington Bridge to China Town
stumbling on a curb on the way.
Blue man skips to the end,
holds up an oak tree; his hands like
steel jaws sink into the bark. His
battle armor radiates off Mount Everest.
I cross between subway cars as the
morning sun cuts across buildings catching
my eyes in its radiance.

Blue man lives in a ghostly blue
at the start of darkness, then he gathers
his form blending with the beginning.

Last night I saw material hardness:
A picture of a classmate who died.

Bye the Bye

I become a star sailing
out into the universe where
I breathe, see, feel. I am beginning.

I touch her hair in the sleep of
distance. She recoils and disappears
unforgiving.

Way out there is a flexing universe
bonding to me, to her, while she
picks out expensive stars.

Christmas Card

On this Christmas card black people
were blacker than usual and white people
whiter than typewriter paper. They were
walking about the mall looking for presents,
looking at each other as if the other didn't
exist. If they bumped into each other nothing
would change. They would bounce off and go
their ways as if the Christmas card was
made for them only them. The card would go
to the right place either to a blacker than black
postman or a typewriter paper postman.
Eventually the card would be burnt up in
an all black fireplace or an all white fireplace.

A Bar

I smell the unmistakable scent
of the living. Lights pierce
through hubbub. Heads move and
squirm in dark color.

Knees pop into view, slide
away under tables; stools keep
company with dresses.

A doorway opens a gaping
hole to evening air, cool on my
confused lips. It seems appropriate
that time skip on pavement,
leap trash barrels, over dumpsters
to forget itself. Wind pushes
me through the door into warm
sexiness. Its slinky seductive behavior
drags me with large hands.

A girl lifts a glass to celebrate
a friend. Legs glisten in klieg lights
creating a moment when whisky, chairs,
tables, drinking all that matters.

A scent of love—moving, percolating.
my body becomes jittery. There's singing
in the back room, pictures of labels, shapes—
black gooey, sitting standing, cashing money,
kissing rubbing noses, gazing…

A tree dances to fun.

Cleaners

Like dead gold fish they
laid on the floor knocked out
by the vacuum wand. They held up
the bed's head board.

The mattress flapped in my
hands and sagged to the floor.
Then two sheets of plywood were
pulled off careening in space.

I didn't see the bedroom floor
only the black cat's frame ready
to be loaded---but first replacing
the red bricks below.

The cleaners had laughed at the old
disabled cat and their reputation,
and had sallied out the door.

Donkey Trail

First Sunday on the job
I saw the pastor mount the stage
wearing a monk's garb of white
with a red cord. He seemed
a flotilla of ships floating from one end and back,
hesitating in front the Steinway.
The congregation waited for a climax
to the sway of white and red. Then
he opened with a blessing.

Behind him the choir stood to sing
a hymn. The music sunk to the roots
of the pastor's hair. He stood at attention listening
to music move up the silos of the organ.
Quietly he waved his hand in time with
hymnal moaning. His wife sat in the back pews
praying to the choir, to the Steinway, to her
husband that the red cord was not too bright.
Satan might be up there dancing with
her husband.

During the coffee hour as we fumbled
for our cookies and coffee, the pastor's
eyes wrapped around me and tightened.
In those pallid eyes jiggled blocks of ice they used
to deliver in the old days.

Elm Tree

The farm rose like a loaf of baking
bread. It was painted a strong red
with white windows and doors.
Beyond, two long fields away stood
the school's symbol, a very tall elm tree,
black against the sun. I would run by
it when doing the cross country race.
In a few years after I left it was
cut down because of Dutch Elm Disease.
Its foliage had a strong lean to the left.
It stood all alone in a large field.

But the farmer was short, wore a very soiled cap
with a short brim. It sat precariously
on a very round head. He loved his
tractor, solidly gripping the steering
wheel and watching both small and large
wheels cut through the earth.

In my last year I took both morning barn and
field work at the farm. I rose early for morning
barn shoveling hay to cows below and cleaning
out their troughs. I would glance at the elm
walking back to school.

One day, during field work, I witnessed
tall angular girl take off running after
a chicken with an axe.

Famous Shed

The shallow wave climbed then
receded. It remembered me when
Tennessee Williams scrawled his
name on the shed's door. Small
unfriendly man, wanting to leave. I
stood over him while he wrote a
play in cement. Karl jabbered away.
After passing the breeze the humped
shadow left flinging a stone at a
tree.

For three summers I painted.
Only one painting survives now
living on a wall in my house-- daubs of
paint flying crazily about a large canvas
but strangely coalescing into an image
of Karl's house.

Like a book the grape arbor closed on
the shed's dark red door. It was a monk's
den inside. There I worked like a giant
moth brushing at a window.

Karl and I built a wood box for
his paintings to be admired in
a gallery in New York City.

He sat on his porch with Helen
gazing at the willow tree, or sea gulls.
I was a pair of sneakers on a bike twisting
in and out of Provincetown summer traffic.

Best Way to Describe the Flight of a Butterfly

My street has a coat of
sun like ants marching in
lock step to beats of a drum.
Even in heat, butterflies cut the
air leaving nothing to my imagination.
Butterflies own space as it comes
to them; they corral it, creating homes
we never see. They build fortresses and
dams, ditches and trees, even the Grand Canyon.
Will they be the last ones to raft
down the river? On winds they swim, assemble
barriers to clouds. They invent their calculations,
speculate if there's a path through woods
they don't know about. Are they in an empty
glass near the road keeping vigil with
pebbles?

Right now there is not much
to see only lines but butterflies make
their rounds cutting puzzles.

I don't have to stand between two
tall pines to tell you how they do it.
Listen—they will tell you.

78 th Street

A humming tower, or maybe
a radio in neutral, or one
of the house cats searching
for a mouse.

The corridor is long with
dark patches in the corners;
a pathetic light in the ceiling.
To the left my room.

It seemed right to settle here
on the seventh floor in New York
City with paint brushes, canvas,
and a brilliant view of the Hudson
River. Its coldness reached all the
way up to my tall wide window.

No wooden stairs to this artist's
garret, but an efficient elevator.
The landlady had two stray cats
and a black spotted dog with sad
eyes.

Kitchen window rose like a coiled
snake. Opaque glass threw shadowy
light on the cats' tails below.

Shades up! Morning pushed light
between buildings, and I began to paint
the great ships plowing the Hudson
River!

Flow of a River

She slumped in her chair;
grasped the kitchen table.
Touching the table with her
face, she closed her eyes,
cringing to ward off the worst pain.

The husband didn't move, examining
a painting on a wall, a clean white wall
with a solitary painting. Maybe he had
seen this collapse and was inwardly yawning
at its significance.

He eyed both of us for our reaction.
The heavy body was feeling the chair
pushing into her as if it owned her flesh,
owned her thin dress.

Leaning back in his chair,
he combed an edge of
the table with a finger.

Forgiveness

A feint glow fell over the
trees. The spire offered
forgiveness. I climbed out of the
wheel chair to the mirror to
watch my stubble grow like
lion's fangs.

Forgiveness and mother didn't
hear church bells. My kiss for her over the
hospital bed died on the metal bar. Then I died and after
that. Not a pleasant way to drive
the streets. Boston yelled hello. I looked
for an accepting light, orange, green, red.

The spire was out of reach, beyond the tree.
I opened the car window for a flow of air
and breathed it in.

Hate

Melancholy is without a face
if I try to imagine it lying
on the grave of an unknown.
But hate has a face in
far flung trees. Hate rips
the earth and sucks the soil. Waits
for the innocent to make a mistake.

In the graves of the dead hate and
melancholy join to spread the word,
and give coffins a shaking.

Hope

There should always be
hope when broken houses
jut their armchairs into rough
weather; when rags of clothes
lie along the road.

Distance becomes someplace—
hanging rubbish, footsteps one on
top of another footsteps, cars stacked
and crushed. In between barrels rats
peeping. Orange cranes lift the dead,
disappear in a furnace.

Out there in a haze there's something
to cling to. Fingers wrap around castles,
don't let go. Even on rainy sullen days
forests prosper.

Before Sunday

My eyes didn't clear to see
the honeysuckle dying, long
angles of it spreading until my eyes
met a pine, a sword in my eye.
Pine needles fell to clouds
of grass. Decaying branches
gasped for attention.

The Parsinage was isolated in its envelope
of bushes and small trees. It seemed not
part of this process of wilting and decaying;
another sword in the depths of land stretching
out like a rambling piece of string. But I
could see its endings here and there in curves
of the road.

It was the sword and land joined
together in a bond that admired the
new pastor's hair seen on a nearby
hill, green with sticks of white houses
separate from a stone well.

Hospital

I lay sprawled. My ankle a twig
snapped in three places. Pain pushed
up my leg. The ramp I built caught my
ankle, twisted it while I slipped on ice.

Four parakeets were whistling as I crawled
into house, called for an ambulance.
Red coated machine pulled up driveway.

The ambulance raced pass poles
and houses, cut like scissors
lengths of highway while sky pinched
my nerves.

The hospital seemed made of porcelain,
welcomed the gurney knifing through hallways,
men pushed me into a bed with a view of a
black diamond, homemade cars,
backyards laid open as a fish. Stolid
green yards murmured grief. Far away
airport beacons.

They took x-rays, drew blood, measured
pulse, wrapped on a splint, then settled me into
a cavernous V in a hospital bed equipped
for climbing a mountain.

With a kind smile a black nurse handed
three spare glasses for reading. At night
a male nurse incessantly talked. A nurse poked
a thermometer into my sleeping mouth. No sound
did she breathe, holding still. In the hall light
I studied door frames my head flat on a pillow.
Nurses laughed in whispers. Outside snow showered,
backyard fences turned into crutches and
wheelchairs.

From my tall glass window evening brings
a ruddy horizon. Church lights come on, its light
climbs to the steeple
Into glossy night.

Quickly, I was wheeled into operating
theater. Waked up with sutras over my
fibula and hastily wrapped splint.

Rehab: A dark yellow room with one
picture. A short bed butted my feet. Above,
a neon light into corners of the room.
In the corner a closet door
nailed with plywood smothered
in varnish. Furniture, elephant like, clogged
the corners popping with flowers.

Nurses raced by my open door.
Patients yelled. Out of the sheet stuck my
broken foot-- Mount Vesuvius. Sheets
held me and I kicked. I imagined walking all
the way up the road. Across the road a large
gold fish.

Wendy wheeled me to the gym. Bodies
lay about in disrepair—physical, mental.
I raised my arms. Now, I too was on the
team! We struggled to wake our joints.
Another room, heads bobbed in a swimming pool.
Outside, a gashed hill with fallen trees. Patches
of raw earth and sky with white lines of a jet liner.
I cranked on nautilus machine watching a ball
jerk around an ellipse.

Long hallways of people in rooms as
anthem played. Wall to wall carpet for
miles.

Sweet nurses catered to moans, yells,
screams, "where are you,?" "get in here."

Caliber van brought me home to
pines with their heavy black arms. My orphan
felt snug in the blue cast of fiber glass.
I counted the days since surgeon inserted
five inch plate with screws and two long screws on
other side twisted into solid bone.
My ankle slowly mended—bone fiber
to bone fiber, nerves finding each other, flesh to
close surgeon's cuts.

I dressed in gym clothes brought by my pastor.
Gray like soot, it ballooned out to go around the cast-- soon
to be a strap on boot. The foot wiggled and stretched.
A ramp was made to go outside in wheelchair.

How Old This Tree?

A day of cars, pavement, building,
nautilus bicycle, Wendy, invalids lifting
weights, climbing fake stairs.

I'm the one riding the nautilus bicycle.
Wendy is sitting on a plywood platform
writing a report on me.

I broke my ankle in three places.
Surgery is complete. I'm in rehab.

Along with the day a tree across the
pavement lies dead, rotting slowly.
The bark has disappeared. It's long,
one end sticking into the air the other
lying on a slope of raw earth---evidence
of a back hoe digging to make way for a building
and pavement. Top of slope is a small forest
of tall trees saved somehow from the ravages
of construction. Their leaves are fluttering
in a slight breeze. I can imagine kids sliding
down the long slope on a board and crashing
into black pavement.

One thing that tree and the invalids have in common,
they're almost quite dead.

I Play Chess

White bishop removed his miter
when I fell and broke my ankle.
A black rook was at my back as I
slid, catching my ankle under a
brick ledge snapping the fibula.

I play chess when I should be writing
or practicing the violin. But I shouldn't
throw it away. It was there for me for
three months recuperating at home.

My ankle murmurs in its blue cage
of fiber glass shaped like a workman's
boot. It's slowly coming back to
life crying "alleluia to chess."

Chess continues to give me the
backside. Too many squares break;
ranks and files drift into bits of leaves.
A foolish rook vacates his square
at the wrong time. My queen gallops
on a knight oblivious of what's happening.
And the king is befuddled. When a storm gathers
bishops jump from black to white.
My king seeks refuge with pawns.

I Witness

On this afternoon with
pollen catching on edges of the
horizon, a crack of light
issues a promise.

Sunlight strikes my doorstep
as a yellow green parakeet
crosses my eyes, feathers soft
a midnight pillow. He might hit me
as light breaks through kitchen
window.

Pieces of belief rush on; trout
scurry for deep water. There's a
prayer in the bow of a wild
goose's neck. Lily pads dip into
scarlet mirrors.

Bleached from the sun, her hair
is tinted gray. Jet liners leave
streams receding to tiny clouds.

What are her intentions?

Or none?

Life of a Tree

I protested the cutting down
of a tree, but David and Clarisse wanted
to enlarge the parking. They argued It
it would not be missed; trees would in time
cover the hole in the canopy.

The tree reached to the canopy
and spread its leaves in all directions.
It had a powerful base that supported
many thick limbs moving up almost
vertically.

I couldn't find Clarisse, maybe basking
in sand on the beach, and David chirped
non stop through his nose.

They began a lawsuit over
my letter of objection.

Living across The Street

If I cross the silky grayness
of the macadam is there anything
worth examining? Whatever is there is
a stranger although I don't think that way.
An astronaut kicked up dust on the moon
thinking it's his or ours. The dust says hands
off.

I see in the hollows velvet curtains long
as a galloping horse. They shatter me.
Rust of the Grand Canyon trickles down
the street.

In a hollow my stepfather leans on
sea wall stricken with fear, not knowing what
to do. I want to help but he is skipping away
on clouds to another world.

I should peer through the curtains to
see if whatever is over there is disappearing into
a story.

What With Meanness?

The sun on the door
are maidens appearing as
if it's my life. Like water
they go. Like flapping wings
they go. Do they see the end
behind this sky or this mountain?

Behind the door the mirror and light
go together but reflections come
in a torrent of fear. Reflections reveal
the giant's yellow teeth and weir poles
bending and breaking, and sorrow crying
in grief.

In reflections I'm stranded as a shark
twisting on shore. In light I don't
deal with meanness or with the dogged denial
of shadows.

We must go like the shark. His value
is ours. But our record of kill will be
our shame.

Indiana

Beside the apple tree, a
shed—windy, old, sprung boards,
dangling nails. Nearby, my mother
and I moved into a house.

Very young, I could only see me as
a glimmer, a light in a forest, disappearing
in wild brush on this country road. Washington D.C.
and thirty ninth street flowed to
obscurity.

The white bathrobe Uncle Billy wore hung
like a sheet on a clothes line. At dinner I told him
about kinetic energy which opened his
jaw in an uproarious laugh. "What is that,?"
he asked dropping his shaking fork.
I opened my mouth but nothing came out.

A tree was pushing against his house. He told my
mother and me about it and about a mournful cry
at night while Aunt Eleanor slept beside him. My
mother's hair was like snow, he exclaimed.

After listening to a talking book, he would take a
walk holding a clothes line. Back and forth,
taking the patch off his eye to clean the socket.

Mother quickly realized coming here
was a mistake. Aunt Eleanor floated about eyeing
her cleaning and cooking.

Country life—feed the pigs and cows; watch the corn
grow, harvest the hay. She walked, irritated with
this life. What will happen to my son---a farmer?
She thought about how she left him standing freezing
in the cold outside a movie theater while she lamented
to friends about her life. Snapped at him when he
Complained.

About how she accused him of killing a ferret for pleasure
when he was saving it from dying in the coal
Cellar.

One window in his room looked out on corn
stumps. They never left him but they did.

Conrad

When I see how big the
room is I think he will easily
outlive me. Ocean spray doesn't
catch him. Waves slide over him,
sand storms blow off his shoulder,
but he's not here. The town grows old
as the memorial proceeds. Sky
intersects with his eye giving me
a chance to gather myself, bewildered
by this event. No such thing as certainty;
even Einstein is wrong about his dice.
My house seems more than quiet
as clouds pass going west.

With trowel in hand and chisel
to granite each day a canvas for
a dream. Cigar smoke turns a shutter
of lights.

I see him on the highway loading
sand, declining, but I don't know
it. How did it come to this—
this grimness!? He doesn't want to leave
but disease shakes the windows!

I hear the news. A newspaper
slams my face.

Making Sense

Dust is forming on words. It
reminds me of the dust bowls
of the West. Dust is forming in our
minds until one day a blue sky calls us
out of our houses to relieve us
from the constant rummaging about
in our minds like enormous worker ants.

Particulate measure days and months,
even years. My time is in counting time pieces along
the wharfs, along stretches of weir poles. Dust
is coming out of nowhere. It's in all these
obstructions along the beaches—fences
for privacy.

It's filling us with greed—robots depriving working men.
Taking breath out of action. It's in the men killing
elephants for tusks.

Marsh

My eyes sweep across a green river—
a violent stream of grasses with
maroon points. If I climb off the boulders
and wade in the warm sea, that would break
the spell.

Barbara sits on a flat rock with Moosie,
our poodle. I feel I am in a beginning
I am in the presence of a miracle
with strange clouds pointing their
ends all the way to Boston.

The line of boulders seem like dinosaurs
lunging in great strides toward the Point.
snakes of heat run up and down my
body. I had just come from carrying concrete
blocks up a steep hill where I was building
a series of walls for a terraced garden.
slouching on a wall, Nick examines the blocks
his wide straw hat blanking out the sun

Seeing myself in the water, my mouth becomes
a straight line drawn by a pencil; and at the tips
of the swishing reeds an eye ogles the expansive sky.
and there sticking out of mud my jaw like that of an
elephant.

Morning Time

Bathroom window morphs to a
haze outside; my face in the mirror
catches the declining edges of skin.
hills are running away and mountains
gallop toward the morning sun.

Strands of my gray hair curl in
the comb, then lie submissively
on my skull.

My face balloons to a rhythmical
sag, snaring lines, while three lights
above smooth out the sink.

Burned tombs of Pompeii wash
out my eye corners.

When I part my hair, sky and
hill make a division line.

New Neighborhood

A strange neighborhood offset by
muscular pine trees visiting with the sky. Sun
in their branches, yellow neighborhood,
nothing could be wrong. Down here
I live in a gray house with long chimney.
my parakeets sing hymns.

This neighborhood puts empty liquor shots in
my mailbox—one shot bang.
They hide in back like a stinking
guest. Years later the same.

A stockade fence appeared at night
growling at the street, protecting house
and grass. Old boards and sticks were
thrown in to fill remaining gap.

Actually, it happened in threes. A woman parked herself
on a guard rail and shot me the bullet stare as
I waited to enter highway. Her magazines must
be jumping with pedophiles.

Centipede

The sun is shining when
a centipede crawls on shingles
peeling out from an old house
its paint scaling back on itself.
In spots sheathing is buckling and
nails letting go. An old man gazes
from its window at privet branches
across the street. He puts his nose
to the glass and holds it still as if
in a reverie. Then he places his hands
on the window frame. He watches
a woman with streaks of white hair
begin to trim back branches leaning
out into the street. Her hair catches
the old man's attention, inspecting
it carefully. She's a short dumpy woman,
and thus is having trouble reaching the
upper branches. The old man watches her
struggle but doesn't move.

He spies the centipede crawling on
the window pane towards his nose. His eyes
move as he tracks the many legs moving
rhythmically across the glass. He brings up
a finger to flick it off but that doesn't deter
the bug. The old man brings up two fingers
to knock him off into the dirt below but
the bug keeps to his track.
Without hesitation the old man raises
a fist and hits the glass hard. The centipede
feels a jolt and his body flies off course but he brings
it back on course. Now impatient, the old man
hits the glass again, this time knocking it completely
out. The centipede is gone when he pokes his nose
through the opening, inspecting the work he has
to do. The woman stops and looks across the
street at him, his face stuck between the muttons.

Our Pit

A great spirit will lift Earth out of
our hands to send it to a
rehab center. The spirit will wash
our hands of the coal-ash
pits.

She stands on its wound celebrating
another year of being in the black
as Earth turns black.

Deep gashes in the land and whirl pools carve
shelves of coal-ash in the earth. Plates
of it emerge, glistening new spoons
mirroring the moon reflecting ghostly pits
flattened by more spill.

Coal ash shimmers, turns bottles of
champagne to mixtures of snakes.
eyes appear through glass as paper
messages; black mud heaves out of
bottle's spout.

Part of My History

Memories rekindle sparks that
remind me of when I hit a home
run the outfielder never found.
when I pitched hard ball at school.
when the morning sun was part of
the relay race I ran and came in
first.

They blend with water---
memories about the almost
deadly fall from a swinging vine
onto a sturdy tree stump that would
have skewered me to death. Or the
midnight bicycle ride with a girl that
meant disaster if drag racers hadn't
turned on their headlights in time to
avoid us.

I don't know where the cliff ends;
but know the unpleasant feeling when
people give advice.

Reflection on Moments

I see hands that held oars
and rowed a boat. That felt the
wind as he cast with a fishing rod,
and gripped a bat that hit a home
run.

I sense the pace is slowing while
the sky swarms with clouds running
for a place down the line. As if I'm
wearing green eye shades, I'm accounting
for the closing door on the living.

Rough spots stick out like
angle irons in a fireplace. Sitting
on a solid school room chair I watch
the commotion of grass as it leans
into the day and brown leaves sifting
their way to earth.

Reflection

Reflection comes at you
when the mirror is you,
not you leaping from a face
card. You stare at you.

Warm light in a forest create
edges and corners of a reflection;
intersecting planes become the
shape of a tall pine. Foliage turns
spring to summer then a Red Tailed
Hawk swooping for prey.

Writing Group

Was it right to limit
the number of pages to
read? Was it a reprisal when
she verbally attacked me in a
restaurant as we were reading menus?
"Yes" to both questions.
Her eyes turned into saucers, flying
crazily about. Where did she get
these ideas that unsettled the group?
We decided to put up with it.

I was dismayed at her demonstrations
thinking I couldn't contain them. They would be
too much for our propriety and then we might
be running for the door. It seemed crazy
like a mob burning torches, marching
down main street. If only she would appreciate
the flowers outside by going to the window,
we would all feel relieved, instead of sitting
upright in our chairs, fumbling with menus.

How Odd It Was

Strangeness comes with the
night tide, clam shells rolling
keeping pace, awkward
currents glisten in the moonlight.

I felt strangeness when Roy, the head
cook, heaved a tall scratched pot.
Where was it going? I didn't look.
I felt strangeness when a hammer broke
down a sheetrock wall, plaster scattering everywhere,
through basement windows.

The oddness of slate forming a
walkway, morning light on blank colors,
gave the impression of a long journey.
It was new to me, a primordial
kid who liked potatoes and not used to
girls. The oddness of the students.
They avoided me—too strange.

Pebbles jumped strangely filling
the path to my dorm. Broken swords I
didn't know existed, sticking up or
laying on their sides. They bit into my
shoes, then I walked faster. Strange
when an upper classman stopped me in some
bushes to tell me that my attitude needed improvement.
My shoulders leaned into the ground unwilling
to listen. I sloughed off what I didn't like and
told the upperclassman the sky and trees were
telling me something else.

I felt tension when I ran the long distance
course, down a hill from school, along a
winding dirt road, past clean white houses
separated by single trees or a forest. I measured
between stones, counted minutes, felt dying leaves
shaking overhead. What was I to eat
for dinner in the huge hall, glasses and plates tinkled,
forks into mouths? From the steep hill on the way back,
I saw black earth and plowed fields. Did I belong?
did I measure up? Was the quadratic equation
my salvation or simplifying a complex number?
Did my paper on Auden cut it?

Strange I didn't notice the dislike of the theater
teacher. Much later in a Greenwich Village café
I witnessed his contempt—eyes in slits and knees
pulled up with his buddies. What happens
to our enemies made or unmade?

I wondered hanging onto a tree
limb like Halloween. A kid forever finding
himself; clinging to nature as though born to
be it. How peculiar to reach the crest of
the hill on the return run and see the school
standing tall on the next bluff. See the sky
commingled with the moment.

Rehab

I did not see the mirror
until a black nurse entered
to check on me and empty the bed
pan. She was nervous as if wanting
to be somewhere else.

I glimpsed at the large furniture:
a highly decorated couch, a bulky armchair
with round rests with exuberant flowers,
And at the bottom a neat row polished nails.

I imagined coming out of this mirror
a lizard at Uxmal—stone face, crawling
zigzag up the wall.

I heard the nurse emptying the pee
in the toilet—"click." She was rushing
like an irritated lizard.

September

Glossy month of September
slips by August, by the crying
days of summer cutting a hot
wound.

Temperatures decline, moments
of coolness when words issue easily.
When promises will cease in a wood.
Something new will emerge and remain
on the brink. Be ready for threats, a house
blown down by a tornado in Arkansas.
Be aware! Touch a beginning!

In this time a chipmunk appears
searching for food; digs holes for
storage and escape. Through kitchen window
I chatter at him praying a hawk won't
spy him.

Top of bronze statue glistens,
signals birds to its throne. Its eye
offers safety in winter.

Stop and Shop

It was wrapped in blue emerging
out of an historical file.
Trammeled on, beat up, kicked
into shapes; left for dead on memory's
bed side table.

Exiting an isle of detergents, I didn't
believe it. He had planted his boots
and tore at his mouth to yell the insult.
Then his body twisted into contempt.
Belly mud flowed out his gut.

Distance was a mile despite these
Letters: "HALF and "HALF," HEAVY CREAM,"
"MILK," "BUTTER". He wrinkled his work coat
to imitate a fish in death throes.

The aroma of packages of chicken thighs, breasts,
and legs comingled with his insult.

My surprise and shock

shattered our friendship!

Store Front in Skibbereen

Owner's gaudy light spread
over people rushing, strolling,
or gawking at displays.

Afternoon light is declining
on a row of buildings leaning on
each other. Windows expose
dried white paint, nicked. Old paint scarred
on molding turn, chipped by kids rubbing
and banging it.

Latest style worn by mannequin. Young women
linger at glass---candy thoughts. Curves of
sales girl's legs are partially hidden.

More lights go on. No emotion only wet freezing
air whipping sidewalk. Door quickly closes.

Straw Blew Away

The town grew in me
like a mold—quietly progressing
beyond recognition.

All threads of the past collect
then diminish. I recognize them
at moments; relive their intensity,
their spark. Then they disappear into
a halo of remembrance.

The town went away in the night, in the
hubbub of summer visitors; in the heat
swelling along the tall wood building
showered in unnatural light.

this feeling weaves between house and
people that I knew who are not what they
were.

I escaped the damage—the flattened town
that once bloomed.

The Club

I remember evening light—quiet
purple making my breath still.
I am in a museum.

I remember the inner sanctum,
a tucked away ancient stove, crusty
burners, tough flames. Windows on the bay
cutting a line through weir poles. Rough
lumber for tables, carved initials, lost
signatures. It might be Noah's Arc—animals
departed, no signs of Noah. Vacant air.

I was there when it made sense—a painter
of the abstract as most of us were. Some a lot
older and wiser, carrying themselves with
quiet dignity as they made their entrance,
a makeshift door slamming behind them.

Artists met together for a pleasant evening
of conversation, drinking, then sitting down
for dinner prepared by a member.

I walk in the billiard room, two white balls and
one red spread out on billiard table. Ghosts of men
whip around table or sit on wood platforms kibitzing.

It's not the painting on the wall that holds my
attention, an unsightly thing living in shadowy
light. I move about trying to remember
where I sat leaning on a peeling wall.
I was behind a long table cheering silently for
those top of their game, wandering in my
thoughts, a pool of uncertainty. Weakness is
in the young, thin glass ready to break; small sinewy
muscle pulling at a tree. I didn't see the
end--pebbles running out in a stream to the last
one. But I was tall even then, seeing darkness
like a gray hawk.

I run out on a sheet of ice to see the club
wedged between two buildings windows blank.
I Still see myself there celebrating the good times.

Temptation

She's there to die in a
wilderness. She sits in a tough
bar watching horizons lap one
another then fade. Green leaves
call out the darkness. She's not dying
there but elsewhere in the brush.
With elbows cocked on varnished wood
she imagines images of people appearing
around her pulling at her dress
or elegant shoes, pulling bottles off shelves,
tripping on her beautiful legs.

She doesn't know where she is but she strikes
like a leopard, cloaked in threads, wearing
sandals; hooting at the top of her voice.
She insinuates herself in conversation,
picking up ideas, thoughts, emotions,
cravings.

At the wilderness's edge
her upper lip is strong but quivering;
the lower is a straight line not moving.
She wants to climb that mountain out of reach
of her long arms. Her nails would break bending
on ledges.

No problem. She would climb using her
silvery hair.

The Effect of Waking Up

It's true the sun shakes the
Colorado River. When I dance
I visit with sorrow. And light discolors
darkness.

Trees seem symbols of shame.
Her clothes are in a terrible hurry
as she walks her dog with short white
hair and black ears.

My bathroom mirror reveals a
ragged face while the wall of gray
railway ties remain the same.
I check to see if my chipmunk
escaped the Red Tailed Hawk.

Green nettles of pines hang
from the sky—blue as a crayon.
Orange fingers wrap around grass
tooth dry.

Slow stepping trees on a slope
rise to the struggle. I realize the top
of a pine is hard to reach with my
fingers rising in increments out
of bed covers.

The Garden

She kneels in her garden
as her knees become wet.
Ignoring the inconvenience,
she becomes aware of a
dark mirage descending layer
by layer to where memories gather.

She turns this way—a cold mountain
rising to consciousness.

She said I should be careful as we
all looked at our menus. What did
she insinuate? I couldn't imagine.
Grinning faces showered the occasion
while she bent forward to view a butterfly
caught between two stones.

We passed around our histories thinking
it would be fun. But she was never without
words, and gave notice our lives were at
stake.

The Moon I Saw

The curve of the pine
is like this moon.
Its waves of light bend on
a wall of railway ties.

Lifting its platter, this morning
sun spills oranges and lemons
on a land waving in softness.

A pitcher extends a great curving
spout while the gold of a harp
shimmers nearby.

Lying open a book calls to
this lonely shepherd searching
ravines for lost sheep.

It's awkward at this hour between
night and day when I'm beyond
this world.

May the night bring soft feeling
and the moon I gazed at last night.

The Present Revisits The Past

My focus turned oblique
from my youth when the sun
reached its peak to her eyes
piercing the land. I then viewed
her clearly retreating to a
sense her world and mine had vanished.

Bland were her eyes; gray as the
bark of an oak tree. Shadows were
everywhere telling me it was over.
She talked about old times, pressing
a finger on each one. Fastening
on the camera, she never lost the
significance of it.

Her eyes filled with tears and she asked
why. She would forget before the next
question. This interview would go all
over the state. That meant sales.

Wallowing in fog the dory would
be on more walls.

Years Ago

I was a green stalk that
bolted out of a flat cornfield
in Indiana. A scrubby kid with
an attitude which didn't change
until I walked the Sahara Desert.

I didn't make a good impression—
backward like a tree stump. I drifted
in the sky as a sea turtle resting in
currents of a turbulent sea.

In fact living in a desert coughed
up oddness. Was it me, the face in
the clouds? Was I sailing with the
birds?

An upper classman pulled me into
A bush and advised me to improve
myself. I kept my cool. Only a few, but
the rest questioned my very existence
or thought of a better idea: a walk off the
end of a pier.

Winter in Vermont sliced the body
in half. It hardened us for life. I
trudged through the snow and imagined
snow drifts larger than mountains.
A sweet girl surprised me with a social call
at my dorm. So rare in life.

I observed crimson sunsets, a gaudy
remembrance of my rooms, KDU, the red
barn, forests, ball field. I do remember
the school cook, Roy, heaving an enormous
pot. Next door was a serious meeting
of teachers and students, their heads
locked in thought.

I recall the aching uncertainty on the
soccer field when the coach burned his
coat with a glare for not knowing my position
as guard. The grass ate my shoes.

I almost cheated on homework, but talons
of a hawk yanked me back. His claws bit.
Never again.

Morning Barn: I woke early to pitch hay
into troughs for dairy cows, their tongues
and teeth snapped at the straw.
I liked the sooty feel of the hay as I dug
into it with a pitchfork and threw it
through a square hole. It was real and so was
rubbing my hands to keep them warm.
I never knew this experience
like sailing alone on an ocean. I
was in my element of long angled hay
and wings of a blue jay.

Time In August

I stick a knife into August
to see if time will prevent me
from straddling two planets. Time
stretches my body like a sailing line
whipping the wind.

Time comes not as a friend
by setting its foot on my nervous leg.
Sea water sloshes over it cold
as a building.

The noon sun makes the dunes
grow red, red as my face. It's odd
but I'm hooked on time.

The door of time appears shallow
but I'm stepping into another world.

Waking

An octopus is swimming in my bed
gently wrapping his tentacles
around my neck and arms. He is
wearing a straw hat with a red band.
Nothing about him is threatening. He's
asleep moving quietly in the water. I
lean my hand to break the seals in
the corners of my eyes, and then lean
back to see what the ceiling has to
offer which is blank white. Nothing of
interest but the gray skin of the octopus
and those floating large cups. I try to slip
away and get out bed but his tentacles
suddenly move to grasped me and pull me back.

Walking In Trash

It is not my doing that
It is dark over the barren plane
without birds calling or making
nests. Our hand has written the
verdict on parchment with
black letters. Ornaments of
the posts of a brass head board
lie out there silhouetted by
the sky.

Even the dumb are seeing
the problem having multiplied
familial existence like the continual
rolling of sand up the shore.
When will we walk in trash out
of necessity while the womb
continues its laborious activity?

The barrenness creates in space
a wound deep in the blue. As the tidal
wave gathers I see myself riding a crest
like a wild surfer working off a hangover.

Drifting unaware, suspicious, anxious,
listening to gossip soothing our bodily needs.

Walking

The owners of this house
could be anywhere, probably
at a yard sale buying knickknacks.
They could be taking a walk after
an argument. Time to cool off.

They see themselves as getting
old like their furniture, or like clouds
drifting around the world searching for a wind.
They wonder what it would be like
To be a cloud drifting forever. Material drifting.

They like the smooth road. Very easy to
walk on. Little effort for their legs. They
will walk to the shore and gaze at the
sunset; see how the sea meets
the horizon. They really enjoy the orange
glow.

West Clock

In the store's gentle lights
iridescent hands guide tiny
shadows just as an electric train passes
under a bridge, its conductor waving
a glowing red lantern.

Is this the clock with a large round
face that grandmother touched with delicate hands?
Its tick is loud like a city siren, bringing
The dead upright in their graves.

The pet dog is barking at its tick
while the morning sun rises through the trees.

Obituary

Going to mother's gravesite is a
journey below tall pines swinging
at their tops. At one time it was without
apprehension.

One time my legs felt strong
as I followed a long road with pebbles
and stones, over a bluff, down to
a flat white stone with her name.
I expressed my gratitude for guiding me
onto a good path when young.

Then my forgiveness.

Then my Love.

I'm another person now. I don't
feel strong in my legs but wavering
below these tall pines. Guilt, perpetual
struggle, the striving to do better. My
purpose became confused.

Am I to be wiped off the Earth's face
in a hidden moment or are summer's
leaves telling me otherwise?
Am I to eat a blatant piece of earth's crust
to chew on till death?

I write, play the violin, tend to my four
parakeets. Does God need me?
I know God is there in a dense mist over
a mountain.

I hope to be mixed with the sea;
to be remembered that I did what I
set out to do.

What People Think And Do

The wharf rises as he secures
lines to the schooner. Water splashes
on his shirt and on the girl nearby.
She wants to tell the truth about
him although she doesn't know
who he is. Tell the lies in his mouth
that have always been there. Secretly
quietly like the sea water smoothing
itself against the wharf. She wants to
step on his fingers; hear his cry
of pain. Soon the sun will turn bright
orange and heat will dissipate. Time
to strike; tell him what a fool he is.

He goes on tying a knot unaware of
her standing next to him. He didn't realize
she had moved closer like a little
animal. He wants to make the schooner
secure for the night which is coming
on quickly.

But suddenly her thoughts move with the
waves she strikes.

Where is the Meaning In This?

I think of him or her living
in a bug infested attic swatting
insects as they make phone calls to
irritate me. The long silences
seep through the line issuing
out my end. I make their day.

Maybe it's a girl hibernating in an
attic, eyeing the dust; waking
her nerve endings about getting a life;
where life fell off and the
attic was the only thing left.

Perhaps she or he is walking on
that sidewalk broken or jammed
against a fence, jamming the phone in
his or her ear listening for the pickup.

Even four letter words with emphasis
doesn't dissuade the intruders.

The snakes followed me to Ireland
breaking the serenity of green fields,
and then back to my new home in Wellfleet.

It's now a stare down or phone down.
Slowly, I'm winning the battle.

Your Move

The army laughs at their
king with ringlets of wood about
his crown. They sneer at his obesity,
his awkwardness at dodging blows;
and his habit of falling into ditches
when a position is over run.

But the king finds comfort in
his bed and books and the narrow
window opening on morning light.

He sits in a straight backed chair
with carved wooden figures
sending the queen to the left,
maybe to the right, or into the center
clogged with war. It isn't his fault—
this slaughter of knights and bishops, and
his beloved rook. And to watch the pawns cut
to pieces.

Reflecting on his girth, his short
legs, the shortage of dish cloths
for the maids, he looks forward
to spring.

Lightning Source UK Ltd.
Milton Keynes UK
UKOW04n1820140717

305268UK00002B/66/P